Little Kisses

PHOENIX POETS

LLOYD SCHWARTZ

Little Kisses

THE UNIVERSITY OF CHICAGO PRESS
Chicago & London

The University of Chicago Press, Chicago 60637
The University of Chicago Press, Ltd., London
© 2017 by The University of Chicago
Published 2017
Printed in the United States of America

26 25 24 23 22 21 20 19 18 17   1 2 3 4 5

ISBN-13: 978-0-226-45827-4 (paper)
ISBN-13: 978-0-226-45830-4 (e-book)
DOI: 10.7208/chicago/9780226458304.001.0001

Library of Congress Cataloging-in-Publication Data

Names: Schwartz, Lloyd, 1941– author.
Title: Little kisses / Lloyd Schwartz.
Other titles: Phoenix poets.
Description: Chicago : The University of Chicago Press, 2017. |
    Series: Phoenix poets | Includes bibliographical references.
Identifiers: LCCN 2016035741| ISBN 9780226458274 (pbk. : alk.
    paper) | ISBN 9780226458304 (e-book)
Classification: LCC PS3569.C5667 L58 2017 | DDC 811/.54—dc23
    LC record available at https://lccn.loc.gov/2016035741

♾ This paper meets the requirements of ANSI/NISO Z39.48-1992
(Permanence of Paper).

For DAVID STANG

CONTENTS

ACKNOWLEDGMENTS

The author gratefully acknowledges the editors of the following publications, in print and online, in which these poems first appeared.

The Academy of American Poets *Poem-A-Day*: "To My Oldest Friend, Whose Silence Is Like a Death"

Agni: "Lost Causes," "Two Mineiro Poems on the Love of Death," and "Music for My Ashes"

Bergstein, Arrowsmith Press: *"If You Lived Here You'd Be Home Now"*

The Atlantic: "Small Airport in Brazil"

Boulevard: "Two Plays"

The Cincinnati Review: "Cut-Up"

Consequence: "City of Dreams"

Court Green: "New Name"

From Three Worlds: New Ukrainian Writing, Zephyr Press/Glas: New Russian Writing: "Fish"

Liberation (Terezín Music Foundation Poetry and Music Project Anthology), Beacon Press: "La Valse"

New Ohio Review: "In Flight"

The New Republic: "Crossword"

The Northwest Review: "On the Rooftops of Iran," "The Zayande," and "Tehran Spring"

The Paris Review, subsequently reprinted in *The Paris Review Book of Heartbreak, Madness, Sex, Love, Betrayal, Outsiders, Intoxication, War, Whimsy, Horrors, God, Death, Dinner, Baseball, Travels, The Art of Writing, and Everything Else in the World Since 1953*: "Howl"

Ploughshares : "Goldring," "My Other Grandmother," "Six Words,"
    and "The Conductor"
Plume: "Jerry Garcia in a Somerville Parking Lot," "Is Light
    Enough?," "Getting Ready the House," and "They Are Moving
    Along"
Provincetown Arts: "Dreams (Gatsby's Beguine)"
Salmagundi: "Little Kisses"

Thanks too to the editors of *Poetry Daily* for reprinting several of
these poems, and to Terry Gross, Danny Miller, and Phyllis Myers
for broadcasting "To My Oldest Friend, Whose Silence Is Like a
Death" on *Fresh Air*.

And with special gratitude to the friends whose tireless readings
and generous comments have been a continual source of good ad-
vice and inspiration: Sam Cha, David Ferry, Alice Mattison, Gail
Mazur, Robert Pinsky, Tara Skurtu, David Stang, Rosanna Warren,
and—beginning more than fifty years ago—Frank Bidart.

Little Kisses

LITTLE KISSES

My mother is mad at the sun.

She hates the daylight—one more new day.

In a nursing home, stuck in a wheelchair, she thinks she's been abandoned.

In the background a woman's nonstop wail—my mother can barely hear me on the phone.

She doesn't know she's speaking to her son.

I have to tell her she's speaking to her son.

"Oh, then I'm not alone! I have a son!"

"Please, don't forget that."

"How could I forget that? ... and you—who are you?"

*

"Are we related?"

"Of course."

"Are you my father?"

"Don't you remember your father?"

"Are you my brother?"

"You're my mother."

"I'm your mother?"

"Of course."

"Was I a good mother?"

"You were—you *are*—a wonderful mother."

"I'm glad you're my son. What's your name?"

"You don't remember?"

"I can't think of it—I'm all mixed up ... Are we related?"

"You're my mother."

"Did I ask you that before?"

"Yes."

"Are you angry?"

"Why should I be angry?"

"Because I'm so stupid."

*

"What lovely flowers," the nurse says, "did your son bring them?"

"Who?"

4

"Your son. Isn't this your son?"

"He's my friend."

I can't stop myself: "Where is your son?"

"Where's my son? What do you mean?"

"Where is your son now?"

"He's dead."

*

"Mrs. Schwartz, your son is on the phone."

"My son?"

"Yes. Say hello."

"Hello."

"Hello! How are you feeling?"

"Much better, thank you. Why did you call?"

"I call you every day."

"Forgive me, darling. I didn't remember."

*

"Well, *hell*-o! How did you know I was here?

This is my son, isn't that right?

You're my son, aren't you?

You came out of my body. I'm your mother.

Isn't that right?

Isn't he handsome—even if he has a beard.

I'm your mother, I'd love you no matter what you looked like.

Wouldn't I?

> *Gimme a little kiss, will ya huh?*
> *What are ya gonna miss. Will ya huh?*
>
> *Gosh oh gee, why do you refuse?*
> *I can't see whatcha gonna lose.*
>
> *So gimme a little kiss,*
> *Will ya huh?*
>
> *And I'll give it right back to you!*

See, I know all the words!

(I probably won't remember them tomorrow.)"

MY OTHER GRANDMOTHER

Her pale square face looks out like Fate—
through a dark kerchief clipped under her chin

with a narrow, elegant pin; you can make out
a white headband under her shawl; her jacket

and skirt cut from the same coarse dark cloth.
The uneven stitches of her hem hand-sewn—

dark leather men's shoes sticking out.
Yet her face has no coarseness—high cheekbones,

high forehead, small nose. Her narrow, suspicious eyes
don't give much away. The corners of her mouth

turn down almost in a sneer. Her private mind at work.

The closer you look, the younger she seems. Forty
dressed up to look sixty? She could be an actress

in a peasant costume—except for the rough
cloth of her thick hands, her long thick fingers in her lap

curling under her long thumb. Her hips seem broad,
but maybe the thick cloth makes her look heavy.

Her sons and daughters—one greedy; one
resigned to poverty and loose teeth; one fat and jolly; one

angry with the world—unfatherly, unmotherly (yet he could
still charm the ladies)—was it from her they

inherited their bitterness? Their charm? Their nerve?

Her only trace, this worn photo, crudely cut out
and pasted to a piece of cardboard.

My father must have carried it with him. Did he
ever hear a word from her (*could she write?*)—

or about her—after he left home; left Europe?
Did he know when she had died?

Her name was Leah—he never spoke of her.

LOST CAUSES

Jacky Searle, 1949–1997

"You learn so many things in your life," she said the day after she learned the doctors could offer her no further hope—

"but no one teaches you how to die."

Rushing to fill the silence that filled the room, I said: "Don't they say we start learning that the day we're born?"

"Yes," she said, "I suppose that's another way to look at it."

*

"Devoted daughter" and "family rebel" (an only child, like you); "charismatic teacher" and "spiritual conscience" (patron saint: St. Francis); activist; organizer; passionate disapprover of her mother's politics of disapproval—

marathon runner in a hurry to get the operations, radiation, chemotherapy over with and get back to her running—

obstinate optimist (your opposite): your cousin; your "*sister*"—

how old she looks since our last visit—

back in the hospital, her face hollow; the dull yellow skin hanging on her cheekbones; the sharp clear eyes in your early painting of her now also yellow, larger than life but clouded over; her hair grown back, but still short, and suddenly ashen—

she hadn't said much—

we'd been talking about TV shows—

*

"Dear Ms. Searle: I feel extremely lucky to have had you hold my hand and point me in the right direction in life. I remember pushing to sit at your feet at Literature, just for the chance to play with the velcro on your shoes!"

*

At 42, against her mother's reservations, she married an ex-priest ("a foreigner," her mother said, "with black eyes")—then moved into a small house two doors from her mother.

"To keep an eye on her," she said ("*It's a mistake,*" you predicted).

"I've always been partial," she said, "to lost causes."

(She once had a plan to turn the White House into a homeless shelter.)

Two years later, she discovered a tiny lump.

*

"She was my rock. While she was running around trying to figure out how to give more money to one of her causes, I was trying to figure out which movie to go to."

*

After each new piece of bad news, she'd repeat: "The doctors tell me I'm in the best possible position."

She refused to get a second opinion, she explained, "because my doctors would think I didn't trust them" ("*I don't trust doctors,*" you said).

Even after her vital functions began to fail she kept asking for "one more treatment."

Quietly she submitted to a parishioner's idea for a hands-on "healing" ceremony (*"She'll try anything, now,"* you said).

*

"She had expectations not only for herself but for us ... in a way, we too were first graders."

*

In the hospital, at her bedside, her mother and her husband screamed at each other about whether she should have a hospital bed at home: *"I'm her mother!"* *"But I'm her husband!"*

Months after the funeral her mother still says: "I'll never introduce him as my son-in-law."

On the morning before she lost consciousness for the last time (at home, in a hospital bed)—

when she finally woke, and her husband asked: "What can I do for you?"—

she signaled him to bend his ear to her mouth and whispered: *"Will you marry me?"*

*

"When we heard the news about Ms. Searle my girlfriends and I just had to go to the bathroom."

*

In the later stages of her disease, she admitted to you (*and to herself?*) how bitterly she resented having to work so hard to stay alive, while "some people" (not saying *"you"*) did nothing to take care of themselves.

"She wasn't the person she wanted to be," you said, "but she tried very hard to be the person she wanted to be."

*

At 13, she wrote about her private world, her "retreat":

> *The beach at night is a somber place . . . a graveyard filled with the skeletons of the beautiful and the ugly . . . no stars . . . blackness far as I can see . . . a cemetery that changes with every tide . . . yet it creates a peace inside me that I have never known before . . . The blackness hides everything . . . I am free . . . Sometimes I feel that perhaps God created the beach and the night especially for me.*

At 13, she wrote:

> *I shall burst if I become even a little bit happier . . . I take care that my back is always to the world.*

THE CONDUCTOR

Breezing easily between exotic Chinoiserie
and hometown hoedown, whisking lightly between
woodwind delicacy and jazzy trombone, he must have
the widest and oddest repertoire of gestures, which
allows him a stylistic and dynamic range unusual
even among today's most highly regarded conductors.
The way he slipped from the grandiose opening Adagio
maestoso to the suddenly jaunty Allegretto made me
laugh out loud. Though his small, complex gesticulations
can diminish and even undermine the passages
where the melodic lines ought to soar.

He's all dippy knees, flappy elbows, and floppy wrists.
Not Bernstein's exaggerated self-immolation, but
little, complicated pantomimes: steering a car down a
winding road, patting down a mud pie, robbing eggs
from a bird's nest (and carrying them carefully away), flinging
tinsel on a Christmas tree.
                                        As a baseball umpire, he could
declare a runner simultaneously safe and out at home plate.

He threw himself into the music—and very nearly into
the first violin section—with the kind of reckless abandon
that comes only with complete confidence and authority;
not so much confidence in himself and authority over
his players, but confidence in his players, and authority
over his material.

These glittering performances: more
dazzle than warmth, more brilliance than magic. Sophistication
without innocence. Does the music ever hold surprises
even for himself? Or terrors?

How much would we love him if it did?

GOLDRING

Getting out of his car one night, he discovers—*No! It's gone!*—the ring he'd worn on his left pinky for more than thirty years.

He treasured it.

Not because an old lover had given it to him—she'd stopped meaning anything to him decades ago.

But because it was an elegant thing: "like gold to airy thinness beat."

The band was etched with delicate crosshatchings—though some of the strokes had worn down to the same smoothness as the inside of the ring.

The part that slid onto—and off—his finger.

It was always a little big for his pinky, so he developed the habit of feeling for the ring with his thumb and pushing it down his finger.

So it would be safe.

He had done this for thirty years.

Why should he lose it now?

*

He'd been having a bad run of luck.

A downward spiral.

Little things.

Like discovering he'd forgotten to record a movie he'd waited years to see—rushing home to see it, but no movie.

He never did that.

An unusual button had popped off his favorite shirt—he put it safely away; but where was it?

Where did it go?

Then while he was inching through a crowded intersection—*BAM!*—a driver who wasn't paying attention slammed into his car.

No one was hurt, thank God.

But he cursed the driver.

And he cursed God.

And now the ring.

He used to feel lucky, but he was beginning to think his luck had changed.

*

He searches around the curb near his car.

He reaches under the driver's seat.

He searches his driveway.

He combs through the trash bag.

He feels under his bed, where that morning he'd tucked in the sheet.

Could it be somewhere in his house, someplace hard to see, a place he hadn't looked?

He sticks his hand down the disposal in his sink.

*

Losing the ring is worse than the car accident.

Much worse.

His finger feels empty.

He feels empty and sad.

One more irreplaceable thing lost.

Another little hole in his life.

He keeps feeling for the ring with his thumb.

*

Endings—separations, partings—always leave him melancholy.

At a party, he's always the last to leave.

Leaving a city he likes, he'll linger on a favorite street corner when he should be packing for the airport.

Or in a museum, looking at a painting he'd come far to see (and might never see again); then peeking back into the room for one last look—then still one more—before finally tearing himself away.

You can't live in a museum.

Or one autumn when the leaves were especially vibrant—crimson and burgundy reflected in an enchanting chain of ponds alongside the road he was driving down (had he ever seen such intense reds?)—he'd have stayed forever; but it was already growing dark, and the leaves would be gone long before he could return.

He has a hard time letting go.

*

This is worse.

He almost asks God to help him find the ring.

Does he really think God can help him find it?

Didn't a missing carton of records turn up a year after he had moved into his new house?

And the book he couldn't find for months?

Even his comfortable shoes (what a thing to misplace!)—they eventually turned up too.

He never stopped looking.

And didn't he thank God when he finally found them?

Or when his father, who couldn't move or speak, died in the hospital the night before his mother was going to take him home?

It would have killed her.

Didn't he thank God for his father's death?

*

So what does he have to lose?

*

But he doesn't ask.

Does he feel foolish?

Or just not want to waste his wish on something unworthy, some material thing, even a thing that was precious to him?

Maybe he hadn't loved the ring enough.

*

He reads elegies—"The art of losing...," "Nothing gold can stay..."—but they don't console him.

Maybe he should write his own poem—the way other poets turn their losses into poems.

Wasn't he a writer?

Didn't he need some loss in order to write?

*

But wouldn't writing keep reopening the wound?

The more he wrote, the more he'd miss the ring.

Would he love what he wrote as much as he loved the ring?

Would he have to thank God for what he wrote?

Would he have to thank God for losing the ring?

*

He misses the ring.

He hates God.

He doesn't believe in God.

He tries to write.

He keeps looking.

*

And what if he found the ring?

CITY OF DREAMS

1. *MASQUERADE*

Should I tell you about my dream? It's a dream
        about you ...
                        your familiar disarray an overstuffed
        Victorian elegance: antiques, bric-a-brac, dark horse-
        hair sofa with swirling hand-carved arm-rests—plush
        but uncomfortable;
                        you're offering me a drink, and
        showing me the score to your latest piece,

        called *Masquerade*.

It's charming—bubbling with flutes, piccolos, clarinets.
        Fresh. Yet complex: sweet tunes you give a sly
        rhythmic tilt; harmonies you save from the saccharine
        with a razor-edge of dissonance.
                                I didn't know you
        wrote music—*could* write music. And though I can
        barely follow a score, I'm actually

        reading yours—listening to it in my head as I read.

I pick up one of the doodads from the marble coffee table
        cluttered with precious objects: a piece of polished mahogany
        carved into the shape of an arm.

                              The hand end
has shapely, arched fingers, with long hooked nails
like a bird's claws;
                         perfect for cleaning under one's nails?
(*Isn't everything here meant to be useful?*)

You say: "Leonard Bernstein gave me that. He was so
helpful to me with *Masquerade*. Donna sang the premiere."

Then Donna appears—her loose corn-silk hair; her white body
   wrapped in a swirling silk peignoir, fluid greens and
   tangerines, almost transparent.
                              I didn't know you
'd been living with her—with anyone. And to tell the truth,

I was still half in love with her myself.

She offers to refill my glass, and pours more of the chilled
   Zinfandel. She's charming, bubbly, fresh
   from her recent triumph at the opera.
                              She seems pleased
to be pouring the wine. To be pouring *my* wine.

You beam. When did I last see you so productive?
So happy?

What am I doing here? It's been a hundred years
   since I visited you, since we saw each other
   last—
         since my pocket was picked, my wallet stolen,
   in the crowd at your father's funeral.
                              No—

that was a different dream …

What do I want? Some help? Approval? I've always needed
    something from you (and you've always been more
    than generous).
                    I steel myself to ask, when (*KNOCK!*
KNOCK!) a sudden pounding on the door (*Who's there?*)

interrupts our masquerade.

2. *THE BOOK OF PAINTINGS*

Of course, I can't remember the artist's name—I'd forgotten it
    even before I woke up. But I certainly remember

    the book of paintings.

I was visiting your house—an odd house, not at all like
    your real one: much bigger, with narrow

        curving staircases and a grassy meadow out back. I was
        staying over, and coming downstairs late

        to a sitting room, where you and some new visitors—
        an older man and a young girl with long

        dark braids (his daughter?), a thin
        blond woman with large gray eyes, a pale man

        in a dark suit (*who were they? when had they arrived?*),
        and your lover (whose name I couldn't remember)—
        were having tea and drinks.

You were sliding a heavy book from a locked bookcase—a thick,
    squarish, clothbound book: the cloth itself

grayish blue and roughly textured. I heard you say
my name as you opened it. The pages were thick

and stiff; you turned them slowly.

I sat down in a large armchair. You crossed the room,
and handed the open book to me.

The paintings were mostly abstractions—globs
        and dribbles of paint swirling up

        out of a dark, grayish-blue background:

        dribbles of yellow, delicate dribbles of black,
        little splotches of orange.

        Full of atmosphere, I thought. *Highly charged.*

Suddenly, as I turned the pages, I began to make out
        faces in the thick swirls of paint;

                then all I could see were faces—the same face!—
                all painted the same grayish blue, more gray

                than blue. Each face had the texture of paint,
                not skin (the reproductions were

                so real, I could almost touch the pigment).
                In each face, the eyes and mouth were wide open,

                like holes in a mask, through which the darker background
                showed through.

I turned each page slowly, often turning back
    to a previous page. Each "portrait"

        seemed exactly the same, the same dark,
        muted colors, the same frightening

        unreadable expression.
        Were these self-portraits?

    Why did you want me to see this book?

I must have looked for hours, while you and the other guests
    (*was one of them the artist?*)

        stood or sat motionless, watching,
        waiting for me to close the book.

        Then everyone moved again, talking as if
        nothing had happened.

Nearly dawn, we all went out into the garden; it was
    chilly, we had to take our sweaters; the sky

        was still dark, but with some color—blue-gray,
        more blue than gray.

3. *DIES IRAE*

6:00 a.m. You're sound asleep, up all night
    in your studio. I'm up—looking for a long-
    overdue bill I'd put somewhere safe

so I wouldn't forget to pay it. When did I last
finish a poem? Or start one? When did we last
have a conversation that wasn't an argument?

Late for work. No breakfast.

Traffic logjams all the way in. And at my office
interruptions, emergencies. No lunch.

A quick dip in the Y pool, to wake me up
for the concert you didn't want to hear with me:

the Verdi *Requiem.* No intermission; no coffee.
Can I stay awake?

The buzz at Symphony Hall: the star soprano—"a little hoarse"—
has cancelled. Better to have gone straight
home, where you'd just be taking out of the oven

a steaming asparagus-and-salmon pie.

Back by 11:00, I'm too hungry to pass up your offer
of a large, rich, aromatic wedge ...

In bed, my ears are still ringing from the *Dies Irae* (and from
a smoke alarm that—was it two days ago?—went off

right next to my ear). Still hardly speaking, we start
the film noir we taped from cable. But

ten minutes into it, I'm drifting off—those insinuating,
joyless voices fading in my ears.

—Where am I? I seem to be in some vast
   space (*outer* space?), a place
   that's not a place. Empty. Blank.

   But with lines, parallel lines, like lined paper
   on which I keep trying to write—only in reverse, white lines

   against a black page.

   I'm shuttling back and forth between these lines,
   bumping against these lines, trying to keep in line,

   while explosions of color—hot pinks, Day-Glo yellows, flame
   reds—flash by like comets, grazing my head.

   Then the lines start closing in on me, squeezing me,
   pressing against me so hard it's hard

   to take a breath.

Suddenly whatever is pressing me from outside
   begins to press against me from within: pushing

   against my chest, up into my skull—as if I had
   swallowed the darkness and it was trying to get out.

Am I awake now? In a feverish sweat, trembling, my
   ears ringing, trying to catch my breath, I tell myself:

   it's only a dream—nothing to fear—not
   the end of the world.

I'm afraid to open my eyes. I open my eyes.
I'm afraid to turn on the light. I
turn on the light. *I want to forget this dream.*

I can't.

How can you still be asleep? I want to shake you,
    wake you up, tell you: *The world*
    is deep—deeper than Day had thought.

    I was asleep. I've awakened
    from a deep dream.

    I have to tell you my dream.

DREAMS (GATSBY'S BEGUINE)

Strange   strange as it seems
You're in my dreams
Still in my dreams

Day   day turns to night
And every night
You fill my dreams

        How I toss and turn
        Will I ever learn
    Does my love deserve all this pain

        My heart's a top
        When will it stop
   Do you/don't you   will you/won't you
        Drive me insane

Strange   strange as it seems
You're in my dreams
You're still in my dreams

Late   late every night
I put out the light
So I can dream

CROSSWORD

For David

You're doing a crossword.
I'm working on a puzzle.
Do you love me enough?
What's the missing word?
Do I love you enough?
Where's the missing piece?
Yesterday I was cross with you.
You weren't paying enough attention.
You were cross with me.
I wasn't paying enough attention.
Our words crossed.
Where are the missing pieces?
What are the missing words?
Yet last night we fit together like words in a crossword.
Pieces of a puzzle.

SIX WORDS

yes
no
maybe
sometimes
always
never

Never?
Yes.
Always?
No.
Sometimes?
Maybe—

maybe
never
sometimes.
Yes—
no
always:

always
maybe.
No—
never
yes.
Sometimes,

sometimes
(always)
yes.
Maybe
never ...
No,

no—
sometimes.
Never.
Always?
Maybe.
Yes—

yes no
maybe sometimes
always never.

IS LIGHT ENOUGH?

Who's there? I can't seem to make out anything or anyone. Is
anyone there? Is that you? In this dim light
that's not light, it's not light enough
to see who's there. I've been waiting for you—asking myself when
you were going to come. Or call. I don't like this
uncertainty, this half-light, this state of bewilderment.
Make it stop. Make it stop before I start crying.
Now I'm shaking, shivering—I want to steady my head against
your chest. Where better to find peace? Wait! I hear your steps—the
sound of your breath, your breathing. Unmistakably yours even in the dark.
Come closer! Find your way into the room. The wind always shuts
the door, so you don't have to. Closer! Sit down
here, near me. Tell me something. Answer me. Is the
light enough? Should I tell you to open or pull down the shades?

NEW NAME

James asked me from now on to call him May—not June.
James May. (He wanted to keep the double stress,
just couldn't stand the endless rhymes with moon
and spoon.) Of course he had his doubts, but not to obsess
over them would be like gardening in Eden without a snake.
In any case, the point now was rendered moot,
since he'd made up his mind to have his cake
and eat it too, and this cake was a beaut—
all icing! Like some rediscovered silent in which Garbo,
like Keaton in *The Playhouse*, chose to play
every part herself: drunk, diva, hooker, housewife, hobo,
queen. And king. The shooting didn't take even a day,
and every costume had a dazzling multi-colored rhinestone
clasp hiding the secret pocket for her favorite cologne.

LA VALSE

"Freedom ends or starts with a funeral."
—Frank Bidart

Death sails into the gilded ballroom in purple satin as revealing
as it is liberating—black ostrich plumes at her hip reaching secretly out to
each dancer waltzing by. Long black gloves. What freedom! What the-
ater!—her feathers tickling the legs and rumps of the previously mirthless
company, stuck in their ordinary, unadventurous if not entirely bourgeois
histories. Suddenly, the whole room comes alive. Everyone feels it, that
instant exhilaration, relaxation, absence of tension and fear; the muscles in their
faces relocating into smiles, their breaths exhaling sighs of pleasure, their daily
rhythms revised. Isn't she, at this moment, a work of art? Lifting lives
out of the commonplace, offering all-too-rare possibilities, insights. Are
we grateful to have this moment of intensity, of momentary pleasure (grazed
by the pain of its very momentariness)? How swiftly she swirls by
us. How easily the dance changes color. How eagerly we flee these enchanting
dancers for the usual warmongers, pickpockets, and enchanting murderers.

HOWL

How'll I learn my lines if there isn't any script?

How'll I find my shoes if I can't find my glasses?

How'll I get to a hundred if I can't get past eleven?

How'll I get to first base if you don't open the ballpark?

How'll I get to Paris unless I review the situation?

How'll I keep the wolf from the car?

How'll I starve the fever if I've got to feed the cold?

How'll I burst Joy's grape?

How'll we make our sun stand still?

How'll we stop without a farmhouse near?

Who'll play with the mice when the cat's away?

Who'll put out the light, and then put out the light?

What'll I do with just a photograph to tell my troubles to?

What'll I do?

How'll I pass through the universities with radiant cool eyes hallucinating Arkansas and Blake-light tragedy among the scholars of war?

How'll I eat shit without having visions?

How'll I find the party?

How'll I get home?

How'll we end the war in Spain?

How'll I get to heaven?

AFFONSO ROMANO DE SANT'ANNA: MUSIC FOR MY ASHES

TWO MINEIRO POEMS ON THE LOVE OF DEATH

1

How could I get tired of studying death?
What a ripe subject, new angles shooting out
according to which hour its blur
darts across my path.

It overflows with all kinds of meanings.
It never stops growing. It grabs me.
It makes me richer. It lives in me like a wild animal
who seems domesticated yet remains
master
        —and tenderly chews me to bits.

2

I'm not going to budge from the gate of this cemetery.
I've already buried ten corpses here in just one year,
and, look, there's another coffin coming around the corner.

I'm not going to budge from the gate of this cemetery.
I'll pitch my tent here, a peaceful tenant, like the ancients
who once mounted their fairs in the same place, their *kermesses*.

45

I'm not going to budge from the gate of this cemetery.
So I won't ever again be surprised
when another friend dies on me.

I'll wait for death,
who once upon a time began turning up here. Death,
who once upon a time started to dig. Death
matins and vespers. Sudden death,
who opens his office daily.
                       My death,
who once upon a time was born
in me, in Minas.

Every time this adagio of Mozart's concerto for oboe plays
I stop everything
put my feet on my desk, like now,
look at the lake in front of me, cross my arms
and begin to levitate.

If I died hearing this music
I would reach the other side so immaculate
angels would take me for one of their own.

How many times did I make these chords sound in the dusk
by the edge of the sea or in my mountain cottage
so the cypresses, the grass, the roses
could wake me with that melody
sounding again within themselves.

One day I'll be dead
and I hope my ashes will be scattered through this landscape
so those who pass will have
the fragrances of these flowers
mixed with harmonies out of eternity.

GETTING READY THE HOUSE

My friend goes to visit his grave
like someone going
to his country house to plant roses.

Some time ago
he acquired this little homestead.
Planted trees around it,
and occasionally he'll go there
as if alive
he could do what he would do only if he were dead.

From time to time he'll see
his death beginning to blossom.
He'll look around, think, straighten something or other out,
then back to the business of life:
making love, eating, inventing projects,
having already left his death
in the place it deserves.

THEY ARE MOVING ALONG

They are moving along, my friends.
I know death is useful in others,
those who put our lives into perspective.
But they are racing, rushing,
leaving their children, their work, their love incomplete,
and revolutions to finish.

This wasn't part of the bargain.

Some leave heroically.
Others in peace. Some rebel.
It's best to leave full.

What am I supposed to do? Even now
there's someone trying to accelerate his own denouement.
I'm not in such a hurry. Death
demands work, work
as slow as being born.

VICTOR NEBORAK: FISH

cold-blooded things
living out their days
in our bathtub
their long slippery bodies end
in see-through tails
their eyes bulge
just as someday they'll bulge out
from their chopped-off heads

they live on oxygen in the water
separated from my room by one thin wall
by another from the mist, dry leaves,
street, buildings, cars
I live with

water and food? crucial
but light from either sun
or socket may not be so crucial

water and food? crucial
but knowing someday they're all
going to die may not be crucial
unaware as they are of their family connection
to other long slippery bodies

on it goes

bodies quivering on the floor
sharp blows flattening their brains
their insides scooped out
and dumped with their scales into the garbage
then they're poached, or fried, their heads
dropped into the soup

no fish is an island
this involves all of us, all of us
processing plants drip with their cold blood
some of us object in poems,
paintings, documentary films
still they make good eating

even while the fish spirits are watching

AFFONSO ROMANO DE SANT'ANNA:
TEHRAN SPRING

ON THE ROOFTOPS OF IRAN

Over the starlit rooftops, in Iran,
echoes the agonized voice
                              of those who only want
to say something.

Not the litany of the muezzins
and their monotonous prayers,

asking no questions, insisting on the same answers.

It's the green song tearing
off the black cloth of the ayatollahs
as if from high above the houses
it would be possible to anticipate
                              the birth of light
that bloodies the dawn.

ZAYANDE ("THE ONE WHO GIVES LIFE")

In Iran there's a river
that comes down from the mountains
with no desire whatsoever
to throw itself into the sea.

It prefers to go to go to go
nowhere
without explaining
its motives for moving.

It races past us
on its travels,
its departure part
of its own brief arrivals.

Like a rushing train,
that makes a home
of each station it passes:
it moves on; it remains.

Transitive verb of being:
to be
is both the being
and the what's-going-to-be.

Lovers families children flowers
have all testified:
the river stays in their lives
never intending to stay.

Where it came
from, it knows,
and knows where it
wants to go.

Though it starts high among the snow-caps,
its ocean is the desert,
and what's waiting for it
        are whitecaps of sand,
        shoals of hard rock
        and bitter earth-apples
        covered with the grit
of a bitter underground sea.

To meet its destiny,
        this river,
                saint-like,
has taken its name
from its harshest surroundings—
stripping itself
of the anxiety
other rivers have
as they daydream
of joining the sea,
—giving up everything
to be fried
in the desert's pure flame.

When others find its path strange,
and go rattling on
about the marvels of the sea,
the river will whisper
to its fishes: Listen—
the desert is my other half.

Who wants to be
just another river
dribbling into the sea?
What a dull way for a river
to achieve glory.
The ocean, I know,
would take me in. But my fate
is this:
        to live within my own limits;
and to make the desert come alive.

It is written into my name.

TEHRAN SPRING

This spring there's still snow
in the mountains circling Tehran
but the thaw has already begun.

Although women are wearing their black chadors,
suddenly you can see patterns of embroidery over the dark background,
a variety of colors springing up on the most daring outfits,
and at any moment
                              from some black caterpillar
a chrysalis will appear,
suddenly one can predict the flight of butterflies.

IF YOU LIVED HERE YOU'D BE HOME NOW

(after a collage/painting by Gerry Bergstein)

Does he really want to be part of this cosmic junk—this magnetic, centripetal sphere sucking into itself a cacophony of fragments: Leonardo's Lady (without her ermine), Vermeer's Young Girl (without her pearl), Saturn devouring his offspring (angry god? hungry god?), anguished Adam and Eve expelled at swordpoint from their homey Eden, desperate to cover their nakedness? They cling to that floating bauble—along with abandoned shoes, disembodied eyes (staring) and feet; fingers holding half-smoked cigarettes; a finger on a trigger (murder or suicide?); family photos—all of it, stuck to this thing dangling in blue-black space from the thinnest filament of wire. (What's holding up that wire?) Would his reunion with detritus be preferable to floating alone in the void, nebulous nebulae glowing light-years in the distance? He certainly seems to be trying hard to reach that cluttered, encrusted planet: swinging like a celestial yo-yo dizzyingly high above an abandoned, littered no man's land from a loose frayed string attached gingerly to someone's middle finger; hanging on; hoisting himself up an inch at a time. Who wouldn't want to escape that wasteland below—even to reach another wasteland?

SMALL AIRPORT IN BRAZIL

9:31 in the departure lounge, nearly
deserted. Monday night—everyone here

is a little too tired to be traveling
to another city. I search for an interesting face

behind the newspapers, and light on
a young man:

maybe 31?—slim and well-dressed (that is,
dressed with some thought): his tan

jacket and pressed gray pants in muted
harmony with a pale yellow shirt

open at the collar (no tie, though there may
have been one earlier).

They fit him elegantly, suit him, suit
his thin, sandy hair and pale,

fair skin. His rimless glasses suggest
seriousness not fashion: a tone

confirmed by the forward gaze behind them—
through them.

He wears a touchingly simple
gold band on his finger, another example

of natural elegance—his wife must
share his taste.

Is he on his way to her? Is she picking him up
at another small airport? Will they embrace

warmly, gracefully, when he arrives?
Or will she be up waiting for him at home, dinner

on the table? Or not—already asleep
when he finally gets in, after her own long day.

Or is he on his way to yet another hotel,
after a week of hotels?

—tired of hotels; while his attractive,
witty, attentive wife, with her eloquent cheekbones

and slightly sunken cheeks,
begins to show her own weariness of

spending so many nights alone.

They'll cost something, these nights.
Everything costs something when you have to make

your way through the world—
even if you're not new to the idea,

or just beginning
not to be new to it.

IN FLIGHT

"Did you hear what I was playing, Lane?"
"I didn't think it polite to listen, sir.
—*The Importance of Being Earnest*

A big, hefty guy next to me, an even bigger guy
already squeezed into the window seat. Big, pleasant
fellows. Strangers before this three-hour nonstop

domestic flight. But they've been talking away nonstop
since before takeoff. Talking business. Talking sports.
China. India (my next-seat neighbor might have been

from India). Talking Cubs and Red Sox (they both love
them both). Google. The Euro. Leverage. Banks. Bailouts.
Masters of Money ("It will change the way you think").

Great deals and missed opportunities. Exxon. Fracking.
Megabus. Amtrak. Breakdowns. Lost luggage and
missed connections. A good place to stay in Detroit.

Neither Cheez-Its nor Diet Cokes inhibit the juggernaut.

So much experience, so many theories, so much
friendly advice. The urgent need to tell each other
everything they know before the flight is over—

the Indian fellow occasionally bumping my left arm
in his enthusiasm. "Exactly!" "Absolutely!"
All they've learned and thought, pouring out.

Pouring out, yet steering clear of delicate subjects: politics
(they know better than that), or home (an hour into the flight,
"my wife" has become "ex-wife"). No names.

Nothing about movies or television. No mention of
any other book. No music. But thoroughly tuned in
to each other ("Exactly!" "Absolutely!"),

handing over and taking in
whatever they can in 195 minutes—
like old friends.

Except not.

As we begin our rough descent, a startling
silence fills the cabin. One of them has drifted
into sleep. Stretching to look out the window

I can make out farmland, roads, then tractors,
and cars. Some bumps, and the sleeper awakes.
But the conversation is over. Shutting down.

Touching down. Each of us left with our own thoughts
of arrival or another departure. Then the busy powering up
of phones, the clumsy lowering of overhead bags.

Jamming the aisle, eager to get off and on
with our lives. No handshakes. No goodbyes. But
separated in the crowd, and each with a little wave,

they call out. "Sam." "Andy."

CUT-UP

Your story was so gruesome, I was afraid it might
give me the giggles ... like in the production of Seneca's
Oedipus, after the king had finally seen everything
and punctured his eyes, the Chorus—however hard they tried
not to—began to titter, then guffaw, and finally just gave
in, gave way, and erupted in uncontrollable howls of
laughter so wild it was impossible to tell from crying.

I listened in silence; in disbelief. Not the punch line
I expected when I asked about your son, your namesake:
a screwup; an ingrate; but hardly a monster.

He'd left school—but why should he stay, when
all he wanted was to tool around with his unsavory
buddies, in the car you were paying for?
You were surprised when he enlisted, and relieved.

Could anyone have prevented what happened?

You were always the cut-up. I loved you
for that, though my father (who had no sense
of humor), most volubly—often directly
to your face (humiliating me)—didn't.

In our little 8-millimeter murder comedy—*Death
on a Ladder*—you played the corpse, and stole
the picture when (unrehearsed) you sat up and waved
after your "fatal accident."

"Henry, what's wrong with you?"
your co-star asked in the school play. "Mama
told you what's wrong with me," you ad-libbed.

Ruthless teasers, we tormented our overweight friend—
who once sewed a dress for a girl in our class he had
a crush on. You insisted he try it on and took Polaroids.
He looked like a Hausfrau; then we all did.

You saved me from my own dull spirits.

We could go for years without meeting, yet still
keep in touch. You told me you'd seen our friend's
obituary: heart attack. Not, you thought, likely.

Stationed in Kansas, your son got married.
You liked the girl—liked her family. Settling down
would be good for him—a regimented,
unimaginative life—the fewer challenges the better.

Who could have anticipated the scale of his anger?
More than once his wife had threatened
to leave. Then he stabbed her. More than once.

And sawed off her head.

No joke. He's in for life. Your lawyer wasn't
good enough. The legal complications have left you
nearly bankrupt. A new lawyer's going to plead insanity.

What else could it have been?

You said your nightmares make you afraid to sleep.
Or wake you up. You were in therapy. On heavy-duty

sleeping pills. Taking early retirement,
you bought a small condo near the prison: to make it
easier to visit. And easier to leave.
"We don't have much to say to each other."

I've taught inmates—some convicted for murder.
Mostly nice guys. Your hapless son
and his grotesque crime: you wanted to know
how much of yourself was in his rage. Could
any possible answer comfort you?

Since our reunion, I've learned you got divorced, moved
to another state, changed your phone number (it's now
unlisted). I've found an address for you, but you
don't answer my letters. How can I help you
if I can't reach you?

Your other two sons are decent kids. Nice guys.
Normal. Funny. A little dull. One wants to be
a stand-up. I heard he's doing comedy clubs.

TO MY OLDEST FRIEND, WHOSE SILENCE IS LIKE A DEATH

In today's paper, a story about our high school drama
teacher evicted from his Carnegie Hall rooftop apartment

made me ache to call you—the only person I know
who'd still remember his talent, his good looks, his self-

absorption. We'd laugh (at what haven't we laughed?), then
not laugh, wondering what became of him. But I can't call,

because I don't know what became of you.

—After sixty years, with no explanation, you're suddenly
not there. Gone. Phone disconnected. I was afraid

you might be dead. But you're not dead.

You've left, your landlord says. He has your new unlisted
number but insists on "respecting your privacy." I located

your oldest son, who refuses to tell me anything except that
you're alive and not ill. Your ex-wife ignores my letters.

What's happened? Are you in trouble? Something
you've done? Something *I've* done?

We used to tell each other everything: our automatic
reference points to childhood pranks, secret codes,

and sexual experiments. How many decades since we started
singing each other "Happy Birthday" every birthday?

(Your last uninhibited rendition is still on my voice mail.)

How often have we exchanged our mutual gratitude—the easy
unthinking kindnesses of long friendship.

This mysterious silence isn't kind. It keeps me
up at night, bewildered, at some "stage" of grief.

Would your actual death be easier to bear?

I crave your laugh, your quirky takes, your latest
comedy of errors. "When one's friends hate each other,"

Pound wrote near the end of his life, "how can there be
peace in the world?" We loved each other. Why why why

am I dead to you?

Our birthdays are looming. The older I get, the less and less
I understand this world,

and the people in it.

TWO PLAYS

I.

A horrific scene: helpless in his passion
for the ruthless but cornered Beatrice Joanna,
who's hinted how grateful she'd be to be
rid of her inconvenient fiancé (she's now in love
with someone else), the hideous Deflores
(who'd do anything for her) murders the fiancé
and delivers the victim's ring, her former
love token—a struggle to extricate even after death.
And so he brings her more than just the ring.

Misunderstanding his motive, she shows her gratitude
by offering him the ring—not the reward
he had in mind. Appalled, she has no choice now
but to submit to his blackmail—then, discovering
a love more complete than any she'd ever known,
recognizes that the ugly assassin in her bed is her
moral twin, and finally, knowing it's too late (which is
what makes this Tragedy), takes him to her heart.

2.

Middleton's best line pops into my head
in Paris, where I'm the target of a familiar scam:
a passerby suddenly stops, swoops down,
picks up what looks like a gold ring, then
hands it to you as if it you had dropped it.

I forget what's supposed to happen if you take the ring.
Some set-up for a holdup?

                  Or that your new "friend"
will follow you, corner you, tell you his sob story.
Desperate. Homeless. Starving children.
He needs your help. Don't you owe him? Didn't he
practically give you the ring? Suddenly, his ruthless
accomplices surround you. There are threats, or worse—
your reward for being greedy.

                  But thoroughly warned
(don't these aces read the internet?), I feel less
threatened than tickled that this ancient gambit must
still work, that some indigent schemer can still
find an easy mark, an innocent abroad.

                    I shake my head.
My predator pockets the ring and slinks away.

                    But they
don't give up. Next day, there's yet another attempt,
which I ignore. Then minutes later, a third (has the play
become a farce?): this time a girl—

                mid-teens, heartbreaking eyes.
And when I laugh out loud, she glares at me
before we both move on.

             Our eyes, however, meet again when,
swinging around, I see her, only a few feet away, offering

the ring to two young Asian guys. Still grinning, I wag
my finger at her and shake my head.

                                Enraged, outraged, she returns
my upright finger with a finger of her own. Why can't I mind my
own business? She's not a joke. She isn't in a play.
How dare I interfere with her work? Who do I think I am?

JERRY GARCIA IN A SOMERVILLE PARKING LOT

Past midnight, a man in his late 60s, tall, with long
gray hair and a bushy gray (almost white) beard,
returns to the side street public parking lot
where he'd left his car. It's hot, and dark, and the lot
is unlit. At the far end he can make out two men
smoking, leaning against the car right next to his.

Alone and apprehensive, he starts across the lot, and
soon catches a whiff of what they're smoking.
Suddenly one of them asks:

"Want to hear a joke?"

Startled, he hesitates, but obliges. "Sure," he says.
"What's the joke?" "OK: What do you call a woman

with only one leg?" "I don't know," he plays along.
"What do you call a woman with only one leg?"

"Eileen."

It takes him a second, he almost groans, and then
begins to laugh.

"Want a drag?" the guy asks. He's just a kid
(the other one never says a word). "No, no thanks,"
the man answers, "I can inhale from here."

This time it's the kid who laughs. "OK. I only asked
because you look like Jerry Garcia.

—Have a nice night!"

"You too," the man answers, unlocking his car.
"Thanks." And all the way home, he keeps chuckling
at lucky escapes, wildly mistaken identities, sweet

dumb jokes (how little it takes to restore his
affection for the city), and at least for the moment
gratefully alive, can't stop laughing—or laughing at

himself for laughing—at his latest temporary reprieve.

NOTES

"The Conductor," in manuscript form, was originally included in the portfolio *For One Boston, Granary Books and Pressed Wafer*, a fundraising project for Boston Marathon bombing victims, edited by William Corbett.

"City of Dreams" is a substantially revised version of a poem that originally appeared in *Agni* with a different title.

"Dreams (Gatsby's Beguine)" was inspired by composer John Harbison's plan to make an opera based on *The Great Gatsby*. He subsequently set this poem to music as an independent song.

"Is Light Enough?": The fourteen end words form a line from Gwendolyn Brooks's "garbageman: the man with the orderly mind." The form, introduced by Terrance Hayes as a tribute to Brooks, is called, "The Golden Shovel."

"New Name": *Court Green* challenged poets to write a Bouts-Rimé sonnet with these given end words.

"La Valse": The end words are taken from a sentence in Jean Genet's *The Lady of the Flowers*.

"Howl": *The Paris Review* invited poets to write a new poem with this title.

Affonso Romano de Sant'Anna's "On the Rooftrops of Iran" and "Zayande" were translated with the help of Rogério Zola Santiago. Maria Lucia Milleo Martins helped with "Getting Ready the House." "Mineiro" refers to someone from the Brazilian state of Minas Gerais ("General Mines").

Viktor Neborak's "Fish" is an adaptation of an English translation from the Ukrainian by Virlana Tkacz and Wanda Phipps.

"If You Lived Here You'd Be Home Now" was commissioned by Askold Melnyczuk and Arrowsmith Press for a set of broadsides paying tribute to artist Gerry Bergstein.